AF334380

breathing space

george mattingly

φ

Blue Wind Press

berkeley

1975

Some of these works first appeared in:
CHICAGO; BEAR; FORTY-NINE SOUTH; THE WORLD; THE SAN FRAN-
CISCO ORACLE; TOOTHPASTE; MANDALA; GUM; PLANET NEWS; THE
MILK QUARTERLY; OINK; STOOGE; P.F. FLYER; TELEPHONE; NEW
YORK TIMES; THE NEW YORK TIMES BOOK REVIEW; OUT THERE;
SUCTION; BIG SKY; NADINE; THE IOWA DEFENDER; THE NORTH
STONE REVIEW; FERVENT VALLEY; OUT OF SIGHT; SOU'WESTER;
CANDY; DIANA'S BI-MONTHLY; ASPHALT; SEARCH FOR TOMORROW;
and others I have no doubt forgotten.

The author wishes to thank:

Lucy Farber
without whom this book would not be here to read

Anselm Hollo, and *Ted Berrigan*
for giving him The Business

Keith Abbott
for editing this manuscript

and the author's many creditors
whom he will never be able to repay.

© Copyright 1975 by George Mattingly.

No part of this book may be reproduced by any means past present or
future without written permission, except in the case of brief quota-
tions used to lend reality to critical prose or other non-living matters.

LIBRARY OF CONGRESS CATALOGING IN PUBLICATION DATA:

Mattingly, George, 1950—
Breathing space.

Poems.
I. Title.
PS3563.A8595B7   811'.5'4   75-5515
ISBN 0-912652-11-X pbk.

Front cover collage & illustrations by Tim Hildebrand, *except* p.31 by
the author, and p.41 by Karen Hildebrand. Design by the author.
Back cover photo by Margaret Ann Johnson. Printed in the U.S.A.
by Braun-Brumfield for Blue Wind Press, 1206 Spruce, Berkeley,
California, 94709, in an edition of 2000 copies, June 1975.

This book was partly funded by a grant from the National Endowment
for the Arts, Literature Program.

CONTENTS

FOR LEE CRABTREE

GIMME GIMME

Morning was invisible,
the highway felt like a bone,
behind.

Hills swell
out of the mind
in the dead of night
sleek as an upstretched armpit
involved with a hidden young breast
90 miles south of St. Louis
between third & high

& just then I wonder
what would you give
to have less than you've got
& never be hungry again?

I'd give this for a start.

O. M. V. I.

In the dream I ate some hash so strong I woke up two days
later mumbling "this is so ordinary it must be happening."
By then I was driving Peggy's car into Denver. Two cops in a
gold Toronado pulled me over. One looked like a real cop;
the other one was cute & had a hard–on. The ugly guy stuck
a balloon in my mouth. "You don't look like you belong,"
he said. "You're right," I said, "I'm just dreaming." My old
friend Darrell Gray stumbled up the road, armed with a bot-
tle of Johnny Walker Red Label. The balloon was pulled from
my mouth & shoved into his. When Darrell breathed, it filled
with fluorescent lower–case e's and tiny parking ramps. They
took us to the station, which looked like a college. I heard a
bowling alley in the background. Suddenly a van pulled up &
all my friends from my whole life shuffled in, denying things
in Italian. A wrinkled detective dragged himself over to a cur-
tain by the wall and said: "All right. I'm Lieutenant Tragg."
He opened the curtain. Behind it was an aerial view of Lone
Tree, Iowa. Lieutenant Tragg pointed his stump at a farmer
carrying a wind–up alarm clock across the street from the
Conoco station toward the Nixon Feed Store. As the farmer
walked, dust rose off the street, covering Lt. Tragg and all of
us. I woke up at my desk at work. It was time for a break.

THE HISTORY OF WEATHER

Blues & rum & big fat
smoke: the Universe
is most of my heart.

As my mind runs into
my hands & my hands
reach into the world,
which weather drives
into my heart, no news
hugs me like you, no
day shines but this one,
even the snow breathes jazz.

BACK IN 54

back in 54
when I was 3
we got in our 51
& drove down 6
to 34
where it was 18 below,
wind from 5 to 45.

we drove 9,037.
Then it was 55.

WHERE WOULD I BE WITHOUT MY WOMAN ?

Morocco.

DEFINITION OF BLACK
for J.C.

The rise of presidential pomp parallels the advance of gas
& the individual is transparent until he drives off the map.
In our time news has tried to beautify many official worms
By holding them up to the light, which makes us look
Further into the galaxies, where light is pure fur,
Fur that eats steel wherever it grows,
Removing the blues from black holes.

There is no morning for suitcoats orbiting backwards.
Once the bums would have rolled off the curb &
Eyed them, but today only rain raises an eyebrow.
I look to erosion to keep you from me, Sheriff, Truck,
Or whatever disguise life gives you
Because it is that wonderful.

Each new transformer makes us walk a little wilder.
The ground we do it all on is built of erased concepts:
Concepts created by buildings that cannot contain us,
Food that goes through us,
Transportation that doesn't move us.

But if there is one space in which things really go on,
There is another space they are remembered in,
And a space in between that leads me to talk.
Though that space may seem to shrink as history approaches,
I notice the trees have moved

A new weather across the conversation.
And black grows ambiguous with orange patios.
My love unravels the warm black sky as she breathes & is
invisible until the first blaze of dawn re-arms her.

The result can hardly be called a result!
For it is the mystery component of every hot dog,
Giving me the energy to result in an apartment in Iowa
Much like the apartment in Chile, where love is amor,
And Boulder is in Colorado, comme ci, comme ca,
Because I can totally fill these pants without understanding
The sky may turn black and mean us no harm.

The best definition of black is this:
Today is Monday. It's not the first time.

The fact that I can't see all of me all the time is the source of all abstraction. The crickets, the cars, the clouds, they're here. So are their songs. But to say that the cars are singing their songs is pure fabrication. Because the noise we call the song is part of the car and part of the air and part of the world and no thing is static. It would be impossible to think of motionless things, or of thingless motions, if we didn't think in language. Rain is really water; the distinction was created (between nouns & verbs, between things & action) so that foundations could be poured for new overpasses & parking garages. This vast gulf between things & their true state of constant motion is why we talk so much, to put them back together. . . . I look at my reflection in the window & think what colors are. The idea of "different" colors is incredibly abstract, though color is one of the great bonuses of sentient being in a material world, because color is so close to thought, and like it, so easily lost. . . . Then for awhile I wonder whether it is more amazing that we exist or that we can amuse ourselves thinking about not existing. But I'm pulling your leg. It's warm, brown, and sliding through my hands.

DOWN THERE

At the bottom of the feeling
was a blank spot
sucking up everything I tried to fill it with.

THE BED

When I woke up I was a bed. My old girlfriend & some guy
walked in, took off their clothes, laid down on me & fucked.
Meanwhile I got hungry & reached for a baloney sandwich on
the night table next to me, but my ex-girlfriend slapped my
edge. "You're a bed," she said.

It was hot so we got what we wanted. A few trains went by & somebody decided to lunge for that gap between the woman & her shadow. We never saw him again, though there was always a giant planet when the doors opened. Of course the pictures that come out of this camera bear down on our idea of resemblance, giving no clue to the sudden faces over ours, big & wet against the sky, but that doesn't make anything add up to more than a day, like any other, out of breath, the breath that is given back when the color of the line on the horizon re-lights the old language. "Maybe" resembles that life. These moments overlap so we can move, & moving, forget. So when I say "do it again," it can't be, again.

AMC
CBS
EVENING
NEWS
with
WALTER CRONKITE

from THE BEAUTIFUL SYNDROME

The President today announced a plan to solve everything
without changing anything. "When a great nation goes bowling,"
he began, "I think it should sail effortlessly through the sky
like a big new machine. If you were in my shoes, you too would
appreciate the urgency of golf & a pliable excuse." Across the
nation, citizens grew deep & away, in the half-light of a weirdly-
glowing President being replaced by multiple vitamins.

*

Whatever had corroded the polls was also eating the trusted aide
as he drank a Black Russian high above the Great Plains,
quietly reconstructing life with Mom in Des Moines. "Come on
down from there!" yelled Mom from her patio far below,
making him grin at The Boss, who fell asleep for thousands of
miles. The Boss's Best Friend, Bebe, later woke him up. "Wake
up, Dick, we're in the middle of plenty," he said as the plane
circled Miami like water leaving a tub.

*

Days go on & off like dentists into tiny holes. Nothing is
blamed, nothing returns, not an old boyfriend or bee-bop, but
jazz eternal. In the lobby the receptionist holds a picture of
teeth in front of her breasts: everything else is imaginary.

MORE CLOCK

I remember being right about something—
was it the milk?

Whatever touched me
I couldn't focus on to touch back.

Experience is just a movie
of the mind mutating:

Step out the door
into that weird dictionary.

TERRAPHONE

Wake up, shake off the bums, light up.
A voice gets a grip on the newly—formed
hand rubbing the eye. Out of which the fan
sucks the day.
                    Today I wonder what the world
calls it. Neighbors chew little chunks of it.
Construction destroys it. I stare
straight ahead at a fast slice of it:
hands on keys, clear glass, bright nurse
passing houses hedging the towering sky
that makes up my mind.
                    Information
is busy. A suitcase limps home. The old bars
are being torn down so we can be shot
into space, scratching our brains with that look
the chickens have, fried.
                    "The South. There
you feel greasy." Grandpa said that one day
at the home for old vegetables.
                    I knew what he meant.

AIR SPRAY

There's no point that stays sharp once it's blown out of pro-
portion, or you are. The light doesn't even try, as evening
reaches our proportions, though we remember how once it
broke the air into movies which made it hard to pretend we
knew what we were doing before. Even the tallest building
bends a little when the wind hits it and a boy bends over to
pick up a dime. But it's not because hunger is so simple that
you look up when I say your name — it's just that you never
got used to having so many parts. The engines have their prob-
lems too, but we just say "interruption in the interruption,"
and go on, because our eyes have to move to see.

(with Steve Toth

GOODBYE SONNET

Outside cool July half an hour from morning
Charlie sends love from Salt Lake / Aretha Franklin
fills the room

& distant trucksounds give life a constant disguise. . . .
Smoke occurs to the plant by the clock:
It's a thought : smoke : to the plant : are my thoughts that
real? Orange drink, for instance, results from
the planter's affection for sharkskin, a few oranges,
& lots of chemicals, with thoughts of their own.

Birds plant their wings in the sun,
Roberto Clemente goes to sleep in the sea.
I dream I am dreaming but everything's real,
the snow on TV & the pictures of you left in me,
though maybe the real you's got your thumb out by now,
in the hamburger storms that drench America
with identical details.

FOR ALL BODIES MISSING IN ACTION

The clitoris was discovered on a dirt road 4 miles south of
Burlington, Iowa, in 1963. It proved to be an astonishingly
efficient & practical discovery. Thanks to its use,
many disparate elements of our modern world have begun
to cohere in patterns more beautiful than the disappearance
of men & equipment into spaces that never before crossed
our minds.

NO CAN'T

I can't feel
there's no *difference*

There's no *I*
can't feel different

No I can't feel
There's different

There's no difference
I can't feel

A. M.

the
human
is
not
in
actual
use
over
most
of
the
listening
area

NOSTALGIA FOR THE FUTURE

Life's just a vast radar
which I mostly go right through
barely able to tell myself
from the information that seizes me.

Gravity : Kiss : Ashtray :
the energy that unzips my pants
snows over the moon & garbles
every country music station on the dial
so people are born differently.

The break in the weather:
sealed with a kiss.
The juice:
pulled through copper wire & confused
in the form of light blowing dust off the beer
in the hands of an angel.

PHASE IN

Greek insomnia
                    should the warm snow
          gag like an oboe
                    proportioned & sad
                         from laughing
                              since money.
Angel elastic,
Your bridges phase me,
You feel like the perjuror's dream:

          Please

          I don't know

          I absorb

TIDE

Branches of blood
                    in our eyes
           hold the world
                          in pieces
              together.

                 Wandering away,
     the warp of distance
                             involves us in time,
         the height of the new grocery store sign in the sky,

                       the postcards

we send strangers

                          far from the depth

of this summer afternoon

                       in the sunlight, curving &

containing us,

                    our hands & voices

         rising

GETTING OFF & ON

Those men up above in golf carts
in whose hands our lives were once placed
have been placed in our lives
so we don't forget to laugh,

so history can burst into tears

& be gone.

CRUISING FOR BURGERS

The radio exploded without a sound. Then the air was filled with hundreds of little weather reports, which landed in the bushes & grass around me & crawled away.

A woman who seemed to be my friend took my hand & said "Let's go." As we walked down one smooth green hill & up another, somebody's mother swooped over us in the air, clutching a purse & car-keys.

She circled to buzz us again, but as she did, my friend put her palm on the top of my head, & the two of us flew up into the air.

Behind us, the mother fell to the grass & got old. She shook her purse at a stump, which growled. Then she turned into wood, and chunks of bark peeled off her face.

When I looked around again, I felt something hard touching my feet. The ground. The woman who had brought me here was waving goodbye from the cab of a big rig. She roared away across the muddy parkinglot, shifting gears very smoothly.

A black man took the ticket out of my hand & pointed to the train. I hoped my luggage would arrive safely.

The train climbed steadily into the mountains. Dams & rivers to the right of the tracks were overflowing. I suddenly looked around & realized I was the only passenger on the train.

The train stopped when we reached a little plateau. "Why are we stopped & why am I the only passenger?" I asked the conductor.

"Express run, mah man," he said, smiling, "but we got to wait fo da flood." He pointed out the window. Down the slope, the train disappeared into deep blue water.

I got off the train, scared some cows away from a field-stone house behind some willows, & walked in.

A calendar said "April" above a picture of a salami. My old friend Deborah Owen was draped over a green velvet sofa, jiving with some black guys in big shoes across the room.

"How long have you been in The City?" she asked, looking bored. "Just got in," I said. I sat down in a big flower pot by a computer terminal of some sort.

Donald Justice came in dressed as a nun in sandals. "Have you been helped?" he asked, pulling out an order pad.

"No, thanks," I said. He disappeared.

"Let's see yo stuff," a big black guy said to Deborah. She stuck out her tongue & pulled up her sweater.

"Your order's ready," Donald Justice yelled at me from the other room. I went to get it so I wouldn't have to stare at Deborah's beautiful little breasts.

Don showed me to my seat & turned on a movie about the life of the blue heron. The sound track was by Pink Floyd — sort of swamp sounds & electronic oozing. The heron reached into the water with his beak & pulled out a cheeseburger. He did this many times, then he flew away.

37

CALIFORNIA GIRLS

It's a nice day on the moon. "Not too heavy, not too sweet," says my friend Dave Morice, who's here with me. "Get back to diggin those holes," I tell him.

He hoists the ten–foot pair of scissors and begins carving out the next hole. "This moon dirt is great," he says, "just like an ice cream cone." I drop a coconut into the hole he's just finished, and the guys with the fire engine move up a few feet & water it. We move on to the next one.

Just three or four plantings behind us, little palm trees are sprouting. "Things grow faster on the moon because of the reduced gravity," they explained to us at the briefing.

After a little more work we run out of coconuts and go sit on the edge of a little crater. Dave takes two Colonel Sanders Snak Paks out of a sack and hands me one. Each Snak Pak contains a chocolate mousse, a pair of tennis shoes, some simulated potatoes, and Kentucky Fried Snails. "The Future sure is exciting," Dave says as he sinks his teeth into a tennis shoe.

The earth is a little smoggier than normal, but still a nice blue, with green & white frosting. I remember a song about it called In My Tennessee Mountain Home. I pop the last snail & start humming & tapping my boot on the cindery edge of the crater. Dave says something with his mouth full of mousse.

Just then a teletype message flashes across the Colonel Sanders marquee down on the floor of the lunar sea: *LAST PALM TREES PLANTED ON MOON. SYMBIONESE LIBERATION ARMY FREES PATTY HEARST ON VENUS.* Neither Dave nor I had any idea that we'd been meeting the latest S.L.A. demand.

Suddenly we hear The Beach Boys singing their hit song, California Girls. The music seems to be coming from everywhere around us in space. "Wow!" says Dave, "that must be the new atomophonic music system they made Randolph Hearst develop last year! Wow!"

The guys from the fire engine have come over, with new looks on their faces. The kids down on the Colonel Sanders rocket-strip are kicking & swaying to the music. Lights are going on & off to the beat in the night-time portion of Earth. Everybody joins in on the chorus: *wish they all could be California, wish they all could be California, wish they all could be California girls.*

from THE LIVES OF THE POETS

After a long evening waiting for John Wayne to blow up the oil-well on Tim & Karen's TV, I walked toward downtown Iowa City in the tiny echo of the last commercial for the Cap Snaffler. I thought it was about midnite, but the bank's time & temperature sign said it was 5:30. When I got to the Burger Chef, there was a huge crowd out in the intersection of Washington & Clinton. Everyone was looking down toward the theaters, shaking their heads.

I pushed my way through the crowd, heading down Washington. Next to a huge jagged hole in the display window of Fuik's Jewelers, Ted Berrigan and Anselm Hollo were lying on the sidewalk. Ted was halfway sitting against the wall, next to an empty gallon of Paisano, wearing twelve Bullwinkle watches on his left wrist & singing somgs by the Irish Rovers. Anselm was flat on his back, looking straight up at the stars, throwing huge wads of diamonds up into the air. As soon as the jewels plunked down on his wolfskin vest, he tossed them up again. A giant baggie full of Colombian Blue hung out of his pants pocket. He was saying *"Aiiieeeeeeee!"*

Anselm's lawyer, Mr. Kingsley Clarke, Jr., stood a few feet to one side, looking grim, in his non-descript but nevertheless weird suit, one hand attached firmly to his red beard. Some little birds gathered on the marquee of the theater next door, going tweet tweet & shitting on the red plastic letters that spelled out *GONE WITH THE   IND.*

The grill cook from Playmore Lanes nudged me & said "It's them poets. They've got the diamonds *and* the dope."

HERE

Talk finds out
who's to talk to.

Thanks to night
we've got wind
to keep blowing
subject matter
out of the way:

Simple pleasure
                    is the only way it comes.

GOD'S WORDS TO THE LAST APE

Now if you stop
& think

the world will become
a solid circuit of seasons
          lips   tears
amazement   and   space

From now on find me
in green roses
& nipples & blizzards:
                    I change.

And listen, man,
          Good Luck.

THE CONQUEST OF SPACE

The sky is an endless home. Its innumerable looks are real only directly underfoot. The one you stand in is about 5 feet high. The looks melt into one immense flat plain. Your feet are in the distance.

Over all this, heat waves lick endless nervous systems. The sun burns down the skin & cloth & ether. It also burns down the vertical darkness that forms the mountains. They seem within, but actually they are away.

Far — far even in this clear sphere, another chain fringes the horizon. And a sharp eye guided mostly by accident can detect a faint scent in that sky. Overshadowing the dull parched bones of intelligence, the bulge of that scent points to the sun. If the scent were fainter, and the impact of skin less violent, you could make a mental line, bisect that line, and draw another line. The part of the second line that passed through the bulge of the scent would pass through the center of the sun.

But your attention is not focused on the scent and only involuntarily on the solar disk. The Near & The Far are just backdrops. Your attention is focused on a point straight ahead, at a little mind propped up on the sand, which is there simply to let you know.

BETWEEN THE BLINKS

As if sunlight were a form of memory
Remodelling the landscape
It occurs to the birds
And then to us

How we get through the day.
If all that matters were not moving
How could birds focus their minute attention
At the tips of branches?

Their attachment to what we take from them
Bends back to include their world
Like the sensation of diving through miles of foam
At the end of which everything will seem

Corrected. Not even the tops of buildings
Duplicate the eyes
In which they seem falling.
And if the next lips I kiss breathe

The pliable sleep of trees,
Then how much simpler airports are
Without planes.
And when it doesn't happen,

The sound is simply carried
To a more real location: inside a mule's head,
For instance, or carried on the breeze
Created by the disturbance we feel

Emerging from history. The siphon of knowledge
Brings us back to these birds
Whose bodies are hallucinated at the same rate of speed
As ours.

(with Darrell Gray

45

Freed by this planet from the need to be huge,
the chemicals grew into colors which amazed them
to life. I can't remember what woke me:
the scenery through which the words are born goes on
so fast you don't have to understand the highway
to be gone. And when you arrive it will seem to have brought you
in one piece. Otherwise

aint. For if you hadn't been born,
nobody would tell you. When the door opens you can be sure
you're being investigated, but relax, give a name,
they won't see what goes through you: a city
is where you grow up, not where you are from: juice
runs stop lights & music but it isn't the light
of light. Someday I will finally put my foot down

& walk away from these little bites my life gives me
to divert my attention from its real business
which only goes on unnoticed. Like the wind & rain,
my temperature goes up & down while I try to make heads
out of all the eyes noses lips hair-do's & looks
of grave concern. But that concern is unaimed, so the looks
are just that. And popcorn must be sold, & rights

to build things in the air! How many angles once invented
don't exist? After all these years of immaculate vision,
I'm just laughing matter! "Life" after "Death"
will have to be called something else! One urge
& all those expensive suits are ripped to shreds, one year
& the stars are closer than baseball. I open two windows:
one for air, & one in case I fall in love

with something that's not yet invented.

CLASSICAL MUSIC

It's beginning to make sense,
being   here   being
here thanks to San Francisco cappucino,
Boeing, & Miss Subways 1974.

The subway lines are very clean
on the map. Abraham Beame is beaming:
he's the mayor of millions of names
struggling to be in a little space.

It's fun   being in New York
a few days — New York, is it fun
being a few of my days? Even cops are fun
in movies or on TV, but must Life
always imitate Art?

My sense is beginning to make
mush out of being here.
Dollars change hands change
being, here. Capitalism can't last,
forever.

        Life is the mayor
of millions of days. Sense
begins to be here. Like the beings
who compose them, days sense
life thanks to space thanks to dollars
& capitalism can't last, forever,
composed of beings being
as lines are beginning.

CHRISTMAS 72

The wind makes me stumbling home to bed
very important.

Inside I take off my hat coat & gloves
& the day's messages float out my head
for somebody who can use them better.

Watching them go helps me see
through the dark the city lights make
around the kisses & yawns
connected to the brothers & sisters
turning lights on & off in their orbits.

This orbit is number 23.
The wind is out of my eyes,
My eyes are out of the wind.

WHITE LIGHTNING

Out of my eyes is gone
but this instant hangs
between your gone eyes
& this new sky I can't hold:
I want you that much.

Each moment is crucial
as the inside of an elbow
as I wonder if I could forget
& not miss the white juice
hung in your hair
that I can never forget.

How pointless the air is!

Your face shooting through me like thought!

SYMPTOMS OF JOY

Sometimes the heart is called the breeze
Sometimes sandwiches are music
Sometimes I breathe
When I can't be everywhere.

The sunshine affords you,
Arms that are sometimes found
In a month of snow,
Carrying a world that can't miss you
As you might miss it

In a mistake though not in a dream.

Actually I am moved not so much
By the engine as by the road.
Even the guy in a fog at the station says
I hear you talkin but you don't understand

So you just smile
& that's why the world is smiling:
At the contraction of long trips
Into short pants
In strange rooms
Like frozen songs
Which have been playing all my life unnoticed
Except for the world smiling
At the contraction of life
Into words.

BEYOND RUSSIAN

Beyond the technical city
is a world that resembles itself
& remembers our lives
as a continual thud
which is Russian for sonar,
Australian for thigh,
and you for me.

When our minds make us lonely
we make up words
such as *you*
and the language I put in your mouth
when you are a dream
rises to meet the language you do speak
that I've never heard.

NEXT

There's a nice run off the roof today, into rings of baloney &
thighs near enough to blow over. Nobody seems to know this
is a century. Looking for the sign of signs, we found signs of
signs & honks. If that's not clear, too bad. You're clear, to me,
and the centuries plant you in a little geography & buzz off,
but not for long, because we turn off the map & rip it to
shreds with the real thing. Constellations, sawdust, slurry seal
& a ramp into what we think next: that's what you find when
you open your mouth: that & visibility, dreaming you up.

ELECTRIC WEST

Everything   pieces
              Failing in any season
to be fascinated or
smile   that electric gush left
in the air we love
like skin. . . .   Unrelated to the night-
ful of shoulder blades, vacations & angular
incisions,
                    In a mirror image
       of the Old West
                    an airplane turns
         circles,

                    distracted forever

for PETER & CINDA & THERESA &
BECKY & DEBORAH & CHIP & LIZ &
SUSAN & PEGGY & NANCY & ANNE &

I fill up my shoe
& the next arms:

Otherwise
I might not know what.

Trees grow out
the road to sun
the pools & the mail
is delivered along
with the news

that each new thing
distracts me

from nothing.

LANDLORD WITH STARS

If today got any longer I'd have to have knives for lunch. It's time for more fluid seas, more edible loans, for time to stop being anything more. When the rent isn't paid, the landlord is reborn in the stars, somewhere, as a flaming career I never wanted. I just like to look: the flesh doesn't get worn out so fast that way, and the plates, covered with the crumbs of discarded stars, careen into the lives of the saints, whose rent was never due.

TO DAY

Fanned by the seizure of my brain by choice
I can no longer act like a perposition!

Out on the street,
the streets are removed: they make a kind of sense
I can't:
          either the engines are between the eyes & the rain
or vice–versa:
                    that's that.

We aren't sure everything's already happened,
but we're working on it —
                              How do you want your burger?
Close to the lawn, says Mom.

                         Close.
               Period,
     I think.
               I think, carrying out the trash,
          that any collection of planets or trash
     is beautiful, if seen from the right distance.

Trying to be at that distance,

     that's what this is.

EVERY TIME

Every time I'm somewhere
Things change

Because sand is really bandaged water

Glare is a straight shelf of light

The bugs switch on their lights

And it all comes back to me:

No wonder dresses get worn!

What a miracle
Today's got a name

THE BEST THING GOING

Shutting the door
doesn't turn out the light

        Retractions say only
        "I don't know how to say it"

You scarf me up like a pilot
I keep my arms blue

        If I say I'm great
        it's because I touch you

ENOUGH

My heart
          has changed

     hands

George Mattingly was born September 4, 1950, in Cape Girardeau, Missouri. After being a child, student, cowboy, college dropout, founder of Search for Tomorrow magazine, typographer, and veteran of the welfare system in Arkansas, Missouri, Illinois, Iowa, New Hampshire, Nevada, and Vermont, he now works as a freelance graphic designer, & lives in the hills above Berkeley, California.

Rowse
737-1190
Canovardens.